# SCHIRMER'S LIBRARY OF MUSICAL CLASSICS

Vol. 231

# PIERRE RODE

## Twenty-Four Caprices

In the

Twenty-Four Major and Minor Keys

### For the Violin

Study-Version prepared in accordance
with modern violin technique
and provided with a preface

by

HAROLD BERKLEY

With a Biographical Sketch of the Composer by
THEODORE BAKER

ISBN 978-0-7935-5133-0

## G. SCHIRMER, Inc.

DISTRIBUTED BY

HAL•LEONARD®
CORPORATION
7777 W. BLUEMOUND RD. P.O. BOX 13819 MILWAUKEE, WI 53213

**PIERRE RODE,** (whose baptismal names in full were Jacques Pierre Joseph,) shared with Baillot the honor of being the most distinguished among the violinists trained by Viotti. He was born at Bordeaux on Feb. 26, 1774, and under his first violin-master, André Joseph Fauvel, made such rapid progress between the ages of 8 and 14, that at 12 he astonished both amateurs and artists by his performance of concertos in public.

In 1778, Fauvel was so deeply impressed by his pupil's development that he decided to exhibit his talent in the national arena, and accordingly repaired with him to Paris. Here young Rode appeared at a *Concert Spirituel,* and his playing attracted general attention and approbation;—one (to Fauvel) unforeseen consequence of which was his desertion of his old teacher in order to profit by the instruction of Viotti, then at the zenith of his fame as a violin-player. Though doubtless intensely chagrined by this occurrence, Fauvel concluded to stay in Paris, and met with no inconsiderable professional success, despite his mishap at the beginning.

Rode, after two years' study with his new master, reappeared (1790) in public, playing Viotti's 13th violin-concerto at the *Théâtre de Monsieur,* as an entr'acte to an Italian opera. This led to his engagement, in the same year, as leader of the second violins in the orchestra attached to the *Théâtre Feydeau*—a responsible position for a lad of sixteen. Here, too, at the concerts given during Holy Week, Rode performed various other concertos by his illustrious teacher and patron, and received his full share of the applause showered on both composer and interpreter; the 18th concerto (in E-minor) was a special favorite, and was repeated by request at 3 concerts.

His career as a traveling virtuoso began in 1794, when he left the *Théâtre Feydeau* for a brilliant tournée through Holland and to Hamburg; he also visited Berlin, and played before King Frederick William II. Returning to Hamburg, he embarked on a vessel bound for Bordeaux; but by stress of weather they were forced to seek shelter in an English port, and Rode seized this favorable opportunity to pay his respects to Viotti (then acting as theatre-manager and concert-giver in London). Probably a hope of repeating his Continental triumphs likewise influenced him to take this step, which, however, proved anything but fortunate, as he was able to appear only once, at a charitable concert, and before a comparatively small and unenthusiastic audience. This misadventure disgusted him with England, and he soon returned to Hamburg, passing thence to France through Holland and Belgium, and giving, on the way, a succession of concerts which added new lustre to his already great prestige.

On arriving in Paris, he was made (1796) professor of violin in the newly established Conservatory. Yet in a short time the taste acquired for a roving life impelled him to seek new laurels in fresh fields; he undertook a second concert-tour, through Spain, and at Madrid made the acquaintance of Boccherini, who provided the instrumentation for several of his concertos;—for Rode, like many other French virtuosi of the period, possessed but a fragmentary knowledge of the art of composition. In 1800 we find him once more in Paris, installed as solo violinist to the First Consul. In 1803, acceding to a flattering offer from the Imperial Court, he journeyed to St. Petersburg, where he was attached to the Czar's private orchestra in the capacity of first violin. His *début* in that city was the first of a series of indescribable triumphs, increasing in magnitude throughout his sojourn of 5 years in the Russian capital.

This was the culminating point of his artistic fortunes. On his return to Paris (1818) the great audience assembled at the *Odeon,* prepared to give their former idol an overwhelming ovation, left the hall disappointed; for, although the same surety and finish of technique, the same breadth and purity of tone, were still his, the style lacked his old-time fervency and potency of expression. This was Rode's last public appearance in Paris for many years; the coolness of his reception cut him to the quick, and, though often giving private recitals, he now persistently avoided the concert-stage in Paris. In 1811, weary of such unwonted inactivity, he recommenced his travels in central Europe. At Vienna he met Beethoven, who wrote for him the great violin-sonata in G, Op. 96.—Spohr, hearing Rode play while in Vienna, noted with wonderment the decay of his style—a style with which, 10 years before, he (Spohr) had been so enchanted as to deem it worthy of his peculiar study and zealous emulation.—In 1814 he married, at Berlin, where he remained for a time; he then settled in Bordeaux, and lived there for the remainder of his days, with the exception of an ill-starred attempt, in 1828, to regain the affections of his earlier Parisian admirers. The acute disappointment consequent on this final repulse hastened his death, which occurred Nov. 25, 1830, at Bordeaux.

As a player, Rode was one of the leading spirits of the Franco-Italian school founded by Viotti, and one of the foremost artists who have ever lived. As a composer, these traits are brought into full prominence; some few of his works—the Variations in G and E, and the 7th Concerto in A-minor—are classics, to which must be added his "24 Caprices," still a standard instruction-book, ranking in difficulty just above the celebrated "42 Études" by Kreutzer, and of equally great pedagogical value; although Rode, on account of his unsettled life, took but few pupils in a regular course of training.—His published works embrace, besides these renowned Caprices, 10 violin-concertos, 3 books of duos, 5 sets of quartets, and 7 of variations

THEO. BAKER.

# PREFACE

For more than a hundred years, the Twenty-Four Caprices of Pierre Rode (1774-1830) have been regarded as necessary to the training of all serious violinists. Notwithstanding the development of violin technique since the early nineteenth century, they are today as essential as ever; for no existing studies are more valuable for the acquirement of exact intonation and co-ordination between the bow-arm and the left hand.

Moreover, they lend themselves admirably to the development of the modern technique of violin playing, and it is with this end in view that the present edition has been prepared. The fingering given is more in agreement with present-day technique than that indicated in former editions; the suggestions made for studying the various Caprices show how they may be used to develop the bowing technique necessary for the modern violinist.

It should not be inferred that the classical technique of the bow can be neglected. The use of the upper half of the bow is as important as it was a century ago. Today, however, control and agility in the lower half are equally important, and these Caprices contain abundant material for the acquirement of this technique. Also, the much wider range of tone-shading and tone-coloring required nowadays can very effectually be studied in the Twenty-Four Caprices, as they call for an expressive style of playing in many forms of technique.

As these studies demand a solid technique and very considerable agility in both hands, they should be part of the daily practice of violinists who are accustomed to playing much more "difficult" music.

\* \* \* \*

These Caprices offer exceptional opportunity for the study of the modern technical device known as Advance Fingering—that is, the placing of a finger on the string in preparation for a note that will be played a moment or so later. Usually, this finger is put down simultaneously with the finger which is at that moment stopping the sounded note. It is as though a double-stop were being played, with this difference: that the note being prepared does not sound before it is required in the phrase. Occasionally, the same finger is placed on two strings, as in the second example given below. The following examples will illustrate the technique:

Caprice No. 1, 4th staff

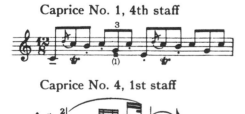

Caprice No. 4, 1st staff

Caprice No. 5, 1st staff, 2nd page

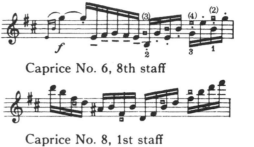

Caprice No. 6, 8th staff

Caprice No. 8, 1st staff

In this edition, places where Advance Fingering may be used have been indicated by the square note ◼ . To avoid over-crowding the page, these indications have been sparingly used. They are merely reminders of this principle, which the student should intelligently develop for himself.

After the principle has become a part of the subconscious left-hand technique, a considerable gain in solidity will be noted in all passage-work, and—because of the elimination of many separate finger-movements—rapidity of fingering will be greatly advanced.

The flexible use of the left thumb is vitally necessary if these Caprices are to be played with an accurate and fluent technique. The thumb should generally incline backwards along the neck of the violin, the joint being approximately opposite the base of the first finger. It is then ready to slip under the neck when necessary to prepare for a shift or a passage of complicated fingering.

Some violinists, when playing in the first position, allow the thumb to come forward until it is opposite the second or third finger. This should be avoided, for it leads to faulty intonation.

Space does not permit a detailed discussion of the varied functions of the thumb in shifting. The essential thing is that it remain always flexible and relaxed.

Those Caprices that are in slow tempo, and the introductions to many of the others, provide a wealth of material for the study of tone-shading and tone-coloring, and they should be practised with care and imagination. Attention should be paid to the varying speed of the bow, the changing point of contact between bow and string, and the amount of bow pressure. The student should appreciate the different tonal effects obtained as these elements are used in varying proportions and combined with the many possibilities of an expressive vibrato.[1]

Where alternative fingerings are given, those above the notes are preferred as being more in keeping with the modern system of fingering.

In cases where two or more tempo indications are given, they refer to the different bowings with which it

[1]See Harold Berkley, *The Modern Technique of Violin Bowing*, Chapter XI; published by G. Schirmer, Inc., New York.

is recommended that the studies be practised—certain bowings obviously requiring slower tempi than others. It should be understood that all tempo indications are only approximate, and that the Caprices should be studied considerably slower until the notes are mastered.

Despite the many technical problems involved, the Rode Caprices must never be considered as mere exercises in violin technique. Each Caprice is a composition of genuine musical worth, and should be treated accordingly. No one of them can be considered mastered until it is played with a clean and accurate technique at the required tempo, with sensitive and imaginative phrasing, and with an interestingly varied tone quality.

## NOTES ON THE CAPRICES

**Caprice No. 1:** The lyric Introduction is an almost inexhaustible study in tone-shading, and much time should be spent on it. At first, the crescendi and diminuendi should be made by increasing or decreasing the speed of the bow. Later, appropriate variations of bow pressure and of the point of contact between bow and string should be introduced, the wider range of expression so obtained being carefully noted by the player.

The Moderato should be played with a fiery martelé, the dynamics being regulated entirely by the amount of bow used.

**Caprice No. 2:** This Caprice is usually played in the upper half of the bow, either détaché or martelé. It should be studied in both bowings. In addition, it should certainly be practised in the lower third, both in détaché and with the bow leaving the string after each stroke; for the fluent use of the lower third of the bow is nowadays indispensable. The slurs (legato signs) should always be observed.

**Caprice No. 3:** Not only is this Caprice an excellent second-position study, it is also a fine exercise in legato playing. In practising it, one should carefully carry out the principle of Round Bowing.[2] The dynamic indications, also, should be closely followed.

**Caprice No. 4:** It should be the aim of the player to make this Siciliano **sing**. The Allegro should, at first, be studied martelé; later, when the notes have been thoroughly mastered, it should be practised spiccato.

**Caprice No. 5:** This excellent study in colorful bowing must be played with careful attention to the expression marks. The sextuplets are always détaché, the quadruplets always a vigorous martelé. The phrasing in the third measure of the second staff, and similar passages, must be clearly brought out, and the dynamic indications always observed.

It goes without saying that the student must have the left-hand technique of this Caprice completely under

[2]*Ibid.*, Chapter V.
[3]*Ibid.*, Chapter III.

control before he concentrates his attention on its musical values.

**Caprice No. 6:** The Adagio is another valuable study in tone-shading. As it is played on the G string, slightly more bow pressure must be used than in the Introduction of the first Caprice; and good use of the varying speed and point of contact of the bow is necessary if it is to be played with the expression and eloquence inherent in it. The Moderato should be played with a broad détaché. The principle of Advance Fingering should be carefully studied in the Moderato as its use will aid materially in obtaining a solid and accurate left-hand technique. To attain this technique, an intelligent use of the thumb in shifting also is necessary.

**Caprice No. 7:** This very fine Staccato study should be practised not only with a firm martelé-staccato in the upper half of the bow, but also with a Flying Staccato in the middle third. When it is studied in the latter way certain passages—such as measures 2, 8, 9, and 10 on the second page—will have to be played somewhat nearer the point if the right effect is to be obtained.

**Caprice No. 8:** Should be studied with the various bowings recommended for No. 2. The frequent string-crossings render this Caprice extremely valuable for developing co-ordination and agility in the lower third of the bow. The fluency of the Wrist-and-Finger Motion[3] must be carefully observed.

This Caprice is especially valuable for the study of Advance Fingering, as it is in passage work of this nature that the principle is most useful, often enabling the player to reduce by one-third to one-half the number of separate movements of his fingers. For example, in the first three measures of this Caprice, if Advance Fingering is used and the fingers are allowed to remain on the string wherever possible, the bow will be playing sixteenths but the fingers will actually be moving in eighths.

**Caprice No. 9:** The Adagio should be played with a wide range of tonal shading and color, and the various means of obtaining these should be explored with imagination. The sforzandi should be understood as stresses, of varying degrees of intensity, rather than as accents.

The Allegretto should at first be played martelé in the upper third of the bow; later, at a faster tempo, it should be played spiccato in the middle or slightly nearer the nut. When practised in the latter bowing it becomes an excellent study in agility for both hand and arm.

**Caprice No. 10:** Should be practised martelé in the upper third of the bow; with a fairly heavy spiccato near the middle; and détaché in the lower third. All slurs and dynamic marks must be observed.

**Caprice No. 11:** This Caprice is in the style of a concert piece and must be played with brilliancy and color.

The lyrical episodes should be clearly contrasted with the passage-work, which demands vigorous, rhythmical playing. The sforzandi in the latter must be treated as accents, and in the former as stresses—the vibrato being used to intensify the stress.

A fine performance of this Caprice is an excellent criterion of a player's technical and musical attainments.

**Caprice No. 12:** Apart from, and also because of, its left-hand difficulties, this Caprice is a remarkably fine legato study, and should be recurrently practised until it can be played with a perfectly smooth and flexible quality of tone. The principle of Round Bowing must be continuously kept in mind.

**Caprice No. 13:** This beautiful composition offers unlimited opportunity for the development of a flexible, singing tone and for control of tone-shading. The remarks on the Introduction of the first Caprice apply here with equal force. The indicated bowings must not be divided, for the ability to vary the tone-color of a slowly-drawn bow-stroke is indispensable to the potential artist. The accents and sforzandi must, of course, be realized as stresses of varying degrees of intensity. In passages so smoothly flowing, a sforzando—as nowadays understood—would be out of place.

A tendency to play sharp in this Caprice is almost inevitable, because of the key; care should be taken to avoid this fault.

**Caprice No. 14:** As in the Introduction of Caprice No 9, the sforzandi must be treated as stresses. The Appassionato, another fine legato study, calls throughout for the technique of Round Bowing, by using which the player can avoid many involuntary and unmusical accents.

**Caprice No. 15:** At first this Caprice should be practised with a firm martelé. Later, at a more rapid tempo, it should be played spiccato near the middle of the bow; and then the bowings indicated by broken slurs should be used. Practised in this way, it is a remarkably fine study for agility of bowing.

**Caprice No. 16:** A great variety of tonal shading and color should be given to this Caprice. All the trills should be as rapid as possible, and each one should begin with a very slight accent, in order that they may have the necessary vitality. The trills in thirds must have an absolute evenness of finger-grip.

**Caprice No. 17:** At first this study should be practised in the upper third of the bow; and later it should be taken in the lower half, spiccato and marcato alternating according to the dynamic indications.

**Caprice No. 18:** This Caprice should be studied in the upper third of the bow, the detached notes being played both martelé and détaché. In the lower third, the détaché only should be used; and at the middle, a spiccato—provided always that an exact intonation has been acquired! All slurs should be observed in each bowing.

Being in the key of F minor, this study contains many difficulties for the left hand and therefore should at first be practised extremely slowly.

**Caprice No. 19:** The Arioso must be played with great warmth of expression, all resources of tone shading and coloring being employed. The mezzo-sforzandi again should be considered as stresses. The Allegretto, also, should be studied with careful attention to the dynamic markings.

This exceptionally valuable study in octave-playing should be studied and re-studied until it can be played with both accuracy and speed. It is suggested that at first, for the sake of true intonation, the octaves be practised unbroken.

**Caprice No. 20:** An excellent study for the development of a sustained, singing tone. All marks of expression must be observed. The rapid runs on the G string call for a consciously strong left-hand grip and for a flexible and mobile thumb.

**Caprice No. 21:** Probably the best study yet written for the development of the "attack". Each stroke of the bow must be commenced with more or less accent, the amount varying in accordance with the dynamic markings. In the short staccato passages each note must be sharply articulated. The difficulties of the left-hand technique demand that at first the Caprice be practised very slowly.

**Caprice No. 22:** The remarks concerning the bowing of No. 18 apply equally to this Caprice. The quick shifts in the left hand call for a very flexible use of the thumb.

**Caprice No. 23:** The position of the left hand is of vital importance in this Caprice. Most of the time the hand should be so far around that the base of the first finger no longer touches the neck of the violin, the thumb lying back under the neck directly opposite the grip of the fingers. For the sake of slow practice, the indicated bowings should at first be divided.

**Caprice No. 24:** The long slurs in the Introduction should be bowed quite close to the bridge, otherwise an even quality of tone will be difficult to obtain.

The Agitato con fuoco should be played with a fiery martelé. The soft passages require as much clarity of attack as those marked forte, but less vigor.

The short trills call for a pronounced bow-accent, combined with a strong left-hand grip on each note. This will produce the electrifying brilliance essential to a finished performance of this Caprice.

HAROLD BERKLEY

# Caprices

Study-Version by Harold Berkley

Pierre Rode

Down-bow ⊓  P = Point  U/2 = Upper Half  E means "on the E string"
Up-bow ∨  N = Nut  L/2 = Lower Half  A " " " A "
Positions I, II, III, IV,  M = Middle  U/3 = Upper Third  D " " " D "
V, VI, VII  WB = Whole Bow  L/3 = Lower Third  G " " " G "

strongly mark the staccato notes.

segue

11872x * See preface

This study should be played in the second position.

Commodo. (♩ = 120)

sempre marcato.

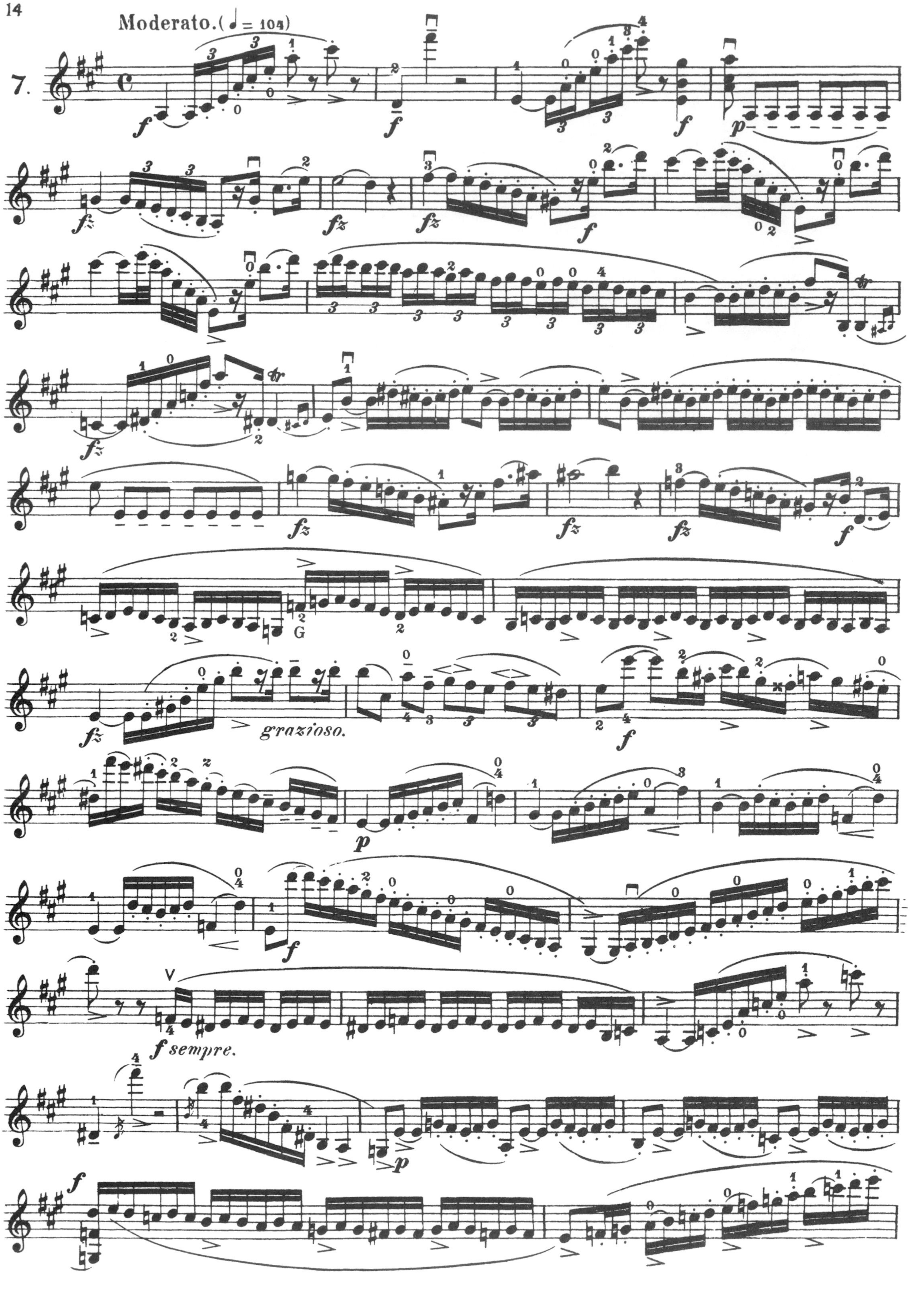
Moderato.( ♩ = 104)
7.
G
grazioso.
f sempre.

Moderato assai. ($\flat$. = 72 [martelé]– 84 [détaché]–66 [lower third])

8.

*f sempre.*

*restez*

di - - mi -

nu - en - do - al p

This study is to be played in the fourth position.

This study is to be played in the third position.

Allegretto. ($\flat$ = 132 [martelé and lower half] - $\flat$·72 [spiccato])

**10**

Allegro brillante. (♩ = 120)

11.

do not take too much bow

Grazioso.(♩=72-80)

13.

Vivace assai. ($\bullet$ = 60 [martelé] – 90 [spiccato])

15.

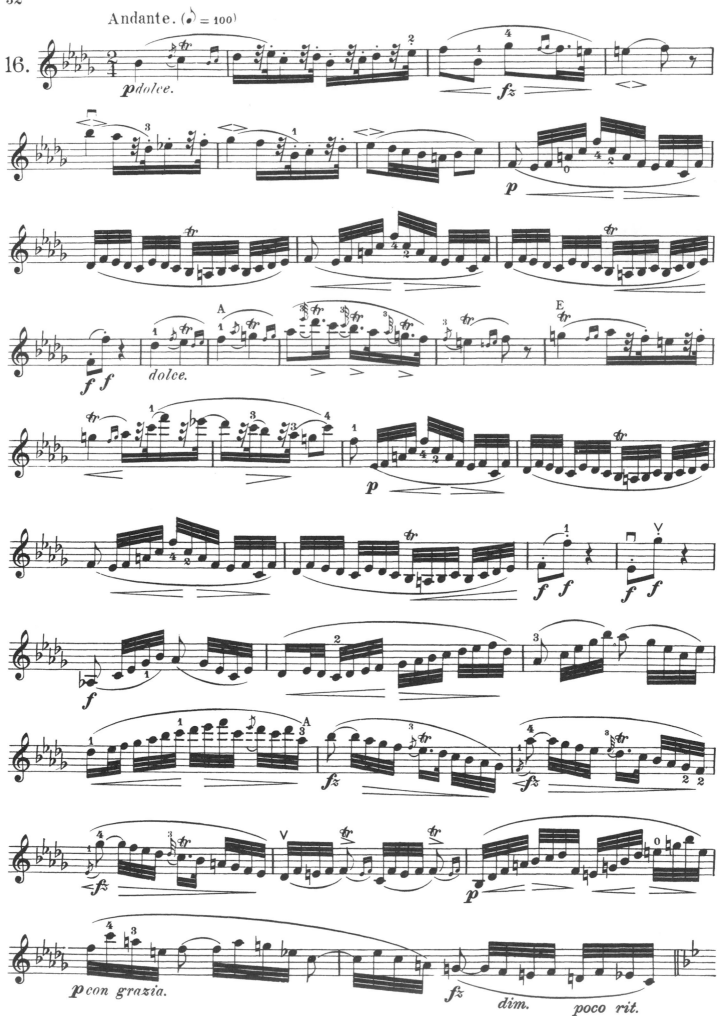

Presto. (♩.=69 [martelé]–78[lower third]–92 [spiccato and détaché])

22.